D1079897

AROUND
ABINGDON
IN OLD PHOTOGRAPHS

AROUND
ABINGDON
IN OLD PHOTOGRAPHS

COLLECTED BY
PAMELA HORN

ALAN SUTTON
1987

Alan Sutton Publishing Limited
Brunswick Road · Gloucester

First published 1987

Copyright © 1987 Pamela Horn

All rights reserved. No part of this publication may be reproduced, stored in a
retrieval system, or transmitted, in any form or by any means, electronic,
mechanical photocopying, recording or otherwise, without the prior
permission of the publishers and copyright holder

British Library Cataloguing in Publication Data

Around Abingdon in old photographs.
1. Abingdon (Oxfordshire)—History
I. Horn, Pamela
942.5'76   DA690.A14

ISBN 0-86299-419-5

Typesetting and origination by
Alan Sutton Publishing Limited.
Printed in Great Britain by Redwood Burn Limited.

CONTENTS

INTRODUCTION

Much of the early history of Abingdon is linked to the great Benedictine Abbey which dominated life in the town for over eight centuries, until its dissolution by Henry VIII in February 1538. By the time of the Domesday survey of 1086 it had become one of the most important ecclesiastical foundations in the country, and was second only to the King as Berkshire's largest landowner. Significantly, the market place (or bury), which for hundreds of years acted as a focus of the town's commercial and official activities, grew up in front of the Abbey gateway. Now little remains of this once mighty monastery beyond a few street names and a scattering of medieval buildings, such as the late fifteenth century western gatehouse, St Nicholas's church, the Checker building, and the Long Gallery, which itself dates from about 1500. After dissolution, the Checker and the Long Gallery were used until the mid 1890s as part of a brewery. St Nicholas's, 'the little Church in the Gate', was built at the end of the twelfth century for the abbey servants and dependants and was always the minor church of Abingdon. Even before the Reformation the poverty of its endowments led to its vicarage being united to that of St Helen's, the town's principal church.

With the Abbey's dissolution, St Helen's became the 'greate resort of all the Towne', according to the mid-sixteenth century commentator, John Leland. It was built on an angle of land between the river Thames and its small tributary, the Ock, and has been described as the finest perpendicular parish church in Berkshire. Its tower, probably dating from the late twelfth century, is its earliest surviving part, but there has been a church on the site since before the Norman conquest. Later, other, non-Anglican, denominations were to make their contribution to the town's religious life. Baptists, Wesleyans, Primitive Methodists, Congregationalists, Roman Catholics, Quakers, Plymouth Brethren, and Salvationists were all represented by the end of the nineteenth century. At the 1921 population census twelve places of worship were recorded in the town.

With the disappearance of monastic power in the sixteenth century, Abingdon had to adjust to a new situation and to develop its own identity as an agricultural marketing centre and a producer of woollen cloth. Already by the early 1540s John Leland claimed that the town 'stondeth by clothing'. But in 1556, when it was granted its first charter, reference was made to its being 'in great ruin and decay for want of repairing'. Under the terms of that charter there was to be a Monday market and also five fairs. The most important of these was the Michaelmas hiring fair, where even in the nineteenth century, farm workers and domestic servants attended to seek employment and to enjoy the excitement of amusement booths, roundabouts, peep-shows, and a circus. In October 1896 the *Abingdon Herald*, in a typical report, referred to the large number of carriers' carts bringing villagers to the town in search of pleasure and perhaps a new job. In the hiring mart itself, set up outside the Lion Inn in High Street, a 'considerable amount of business and preliminary higgling' was under way by 11 a.m. Men wanting work as carters wore a piece of whipcord to indicate their trade, and when they had obtained a hiring they added some ribbon to indicate that they no longer sought employment. They were then free to spend the rest of the day at the menagerie and circus, or the peep-show, with its 'views of the latest horrors', or they could admire such special attractions as a 'boxing lion'.

Agriculture was the basis of Abingdon's trade and prosperity up to the twentieth century, with the malt trade already well established in monastic times. Although woollen cloth manufacture declined as a result of the spread of cloth industries elsewhere, partial compensation for this was secured in the nineteenth century by the growth of a large-scale business in cheap ready-made clothes – trousers, jackets, smocks, and the like. In 1864 a local trade directory referred to the firm of Hyde, Son & Clarke (later Clarke, Sons & Co.) as one of the biggest manufacturers of clothing in the country. Often the garments were made up by women working in their own home, either in Abingdon itself or in villages like Sutton Courtenay and Drayton, within a six to eight mile radius of the town. In 1864 the firm employed around 1,850 workers, 350 of them in its West St Helen Street factory and the remaining 1,500 in their own homes. Each of these outworkers had to collect the cut-out garments from the factory and arrange for their return when the work was completed. By the end of the century the labour force had increased to about 2,000 and even now local people can remember their mother or grandmother collecting bundles of twelve garments from the factory and pushing them home in an old pram to be sewn up on a treadle sewing machine. In the 1890s they received 2¼d to 3½d (about 1p to 2p) per pair for finishing trousers, and out of this they had to pay for their own cotton and thread!

The firm's main driving force was John Creemer Clarke, a Devonian by birth and an active Wesleyan Methodist. He was largely responsible for building the Trinity Methodist church and school at the corner of Park Road and Conduit Road and for financing the construction of the town's first cottage hospital, opened in 1886. He was also destined to be the borough's last MP, holding the seat for the Liberals from 1874 to 1885, when boundary reorganisation led to its being included in the North Berkshire constituency. When he died in February 1895, his estate was valued at the then substantial sum of about £85,000. Clarke's continued in business until around 1932, when they went into voluntary liquidation. At that stage the liquidator was able to dispose of the factory as a going concern, but in the following year economic depression and the prosecution of one of the firm's former directors for fraud proved too much and the business finally collapsed.

Another major nineteenth century enterprise was that of Morland's brewery. Brewing was long-established in Abingdon, with nine brewers recorded in the mid 1580s and many more by the eighteenth century. Morland's moved to the town from their West Ilsley base in 1861, when Edward Henry Morland purchased the Eagle brewery in Ock Street. This is still the centre of the firm's operations in the town. Another Abingdon brewery, The Abbey, was quickly absorbed, and its cellars continued to be used for many years. Interestingly, in the mid 1890s, the town had 35 public houses and 10 beer retailers for a population of under 7,000 – a signal tribute to the inhabitants' beer-drinking propensities.

Other trades included the manufacture of sail-cloth, sacking and ropes, which prospered particularly during the wars with France from 1793 to 1815, the manufacture of mats and carpets, and the production of leather. In 1879 the Abingdon Carpet Manufacturing Company was founded by the Shepherd brothers as an extension of their jute weaving business, and by the end of the century their factory at Thames Wharf was making mats and carpets of cocoa fibre, Thames rushes, jute and wool. Unfortunately foreign competition after the First World War undermined their prosperity and the firm ceased operations at the beginning of the 1930s.

In the second and third quarters of the nineteenth century there was also an important paper-making business run by John Thomas Norris at Sutton Courtenay. As early as 1840 it employed about twenty-five people but by the beginning of the 1870s it had a labour force of 41 males and 21 females in the village alone. Its production ended in the early 1880s, about a decade after Mr Norris's death. Like John Creemer Clarke, he combined business with politics, being Liberal MP for Abingdon from 1857 to 1865.

In the twentieth century a much-needed boost was given to the town's commercial prospects by the opening in September 1929 of the MG car factory, in what had been part of the Pavlova leather factory in Cemetery road. Employees increased from around a hundred soon after its opening to about 1,200 in 1978, and it won a world-wide reputation for its high quality sports cars. In the late 1970s about 50,000 to 60,000 cars a year were being produced. The factory was closed in October 1980 as part of BL Cars' reorganisation plans, and demolition of some of the premises began soon after.

From the early 1930s the Royal Air Force base at Shippon similarly contributed to the economic and social life of the area. RAF Abingdon was opened on 1

September, 1932, with four officers, one warrant-officer, eight NCOs and 42 airmen. Fifty years later these had increased to 73 officers, 279 warrant-officers and senior NCOs, and 821 airmen and airwomen (to say nothing of civilian employees.) In April 1955 officers and men were given the Freedom of the Borough, with the privilege of marching through the streets on 'all Ceremonial Occasions with Bayonets Fixed, Colours Flying, Drums Beating and Bands Playing'.

Yet, despite these developments, during the nineteenth century, in particular, Abingdon largely stagnated. Between 1801 and 1901, whilst the population of England and Wales almost quadrupled, the borough's own inhabitants increased by only about a half – from 4,356 to 6, 480. Even in 1931 they still numbered only 7,829, and it was not until after the Second World War, with the building of new housing estates on the fringes of the town, that a major expansion took place. In 1981 there was a population of 22,862.

For centuries the Thames provided a vital trading and communications link with the outside world. Even the stones used to build the Abbey came by water, while in the 1620s writers commented on the heavy malt traffic despatched by water *en route* for London. Grain, wool, and some manufactured goods also went by river barge, the journey to the capital's wharves taking four or five days according to the state of the water, and the return trip, against the current, lasting perhaps seven to ten days.

In September 1810 these commercial links were widened with the coming of the Wilts and Berks canal. By the late 1830s Abingdon's coal wharf was described as the busiest on the eastern portion of that waterway, and the borough had become the centre of a waterways network linking Bristol, London, Birmingham and the Black Country.

However, in 1837–38 the corporation made a fatal error in refusing to allow the main line of the Great Western Railway to run through the town. Although it soon repented, by then it was too late. At first Abingdonians wishing to travel by train had to go by road to Culham or Steventon, in order to pick up a connection. Then in May 1856, a branch line, built privately by the Abingdon Railway Company, linked the town to the main line system, first at a junction in Culham parish and later, in 1873, by means of a new station at Radley. But it proved a poor substitute for direct access, even though the GWR undertook to run it. The Abingdon Company survived to 1904, when its shareholders were offered £20 of GWR Ordinary Stock for each £10 holding they had in the local enterprise. The line was closed to passenger traffic in September 1963, and the station itself has since been demolished, with the area currently scheduled for redevelopment. The canal also became less popular in Victorian times, thanks to rail competition, and it was eventually abandoned in 1906, after an embankment collapsed. Three years later an official report commented that the stagnant state of its water made it 'offensive to the people of . . . Abingdon'. The canal company went out of business in 1914, and its former waterways were gradually drained and filled in.

Meanwhile the disadvantages of the town's lack of a direct link with the general rail network were already apparent in 1859 when the *Quarterly Review* referred to it as 'a quiet melancholy old place, rather going astern in these competitive days'. Four years later the former landlord of the Crown and Thistle Hotel confirmed this gloomy picture when he contrasted conditions in the 1860s with those in the 'good old days' before the railways. Then, at assizes, quarter sessions, and race-meeting times, he had often 'paid as much as £50 for beds out of the house, but rarely of late years had he had occasion to require one'. Soon further blows were to fall.

Throughout the first half of the nineteenth century Abingdon corporation had successfully defended the borough's ancient status as the capital of Berkshire. But in the late 1860s the battle was lost to its more dynamic rival, Reading. Despite protests, in January 1868, the county magistrates decided the town's gaol (opened in 1811 and built at a cost of £26,000) was no longer to be used. Prisoners were, instead, transferred to Reading. The following year Abingdon ceased to be an assize town, and in 1874 the gaol premises were sold to John Creemer Clarke for just over £2,500. He, in turn, disposed of them for about £2,000 in 1880 to Charles Woodbridge, a saddler and corn dealer, who used part of them for his business. Other sections were converted into tenement dwellings.

The closure of the town's race-meetings in 1875 further undermined its social status. During the eighteenth century, the races, held at Culham Heath, had attracted a brilliant assembly of visitors. Balls and concerts were arranged in the elegant seventeenth century Town Hall to entertain them, and cock-fights were organised at the New Inn (later the Queen's Arms Hotel) to add to the general excitement. But by the 1870s those heady days had long since faded away. A local writer, James Townsend, in 1910 referred to Abingdon as 'not wealthy, but picturesque and good to live in'.

Early in the present century efforts were made to promote the town as a holiday resort, offering opportunities for excursions by river, road, and rail. 'Visitors invariably declare their delight with their most charming holiday, and many return year after year', declared an official guide in about 1920. Over sixty years later some of that holiday atmosphere remains, especially beside the river, where pleasure craft of all kinds line the banks during the summer months.

But it is as an expanding residential and business centre that Abingdon's future seemingly lies. Not only has there been a growth of industrial and trading estates, but housing demand has been boosted by the post-1945 expansion of the Atomic Energy Research Establishment at nearby Harwell. More recently, the JET (Joint European Torus) project at Culham has reinforced that trend, while through Didcot railway station the town is brought within easy commuting distance of London. Abingdon is no longer the rural marketing centre it was when most of the photographs in this book were taken. They are a haunting reminder of how much life has changed in the area since the end of the Second World War, as well as an indication of where the continuities can still be found.

NB: The reference to Pevsner in some captions is to Sir Nikolaus Pevsner's *Berkshire* (Penguin Books, 1966 edn.). The names in brackets after certain captions are of those who have provided the illustrations in question.

Streets and Buildings

Market Place, Abingdon.

THE MARKET PLACE, C .1900, with the Town (or County) Hall. This was erected between 1678 and 1682 to serve as an Assize Court and Market House. It was constructed under the direction of Christopher Kempster of Burford, who had worked with Sir Christopher Wren on St Paul's Cathedral in London. It cost £2,772 to build and was described by the late-seventeenth century traveller, Celia Fiennes, as the finest market house in England. When the Assizes were removed to Reading in 1869 the building was used as a market house, corn exchange, and, from 1931, as the town museum – a role it still fulfils. To the rear of the photograph, the narrow northern entrance to Bridge Street was widened by the demolition of the shop at No. 4 Bridge Street and other property in 1937/38. Alfred H. Simpson's outfitter's shop (now Shepherd and Simpson's) still remains at the corner of the Market Place and Bridge Street, although its windows are much changed. In 1900, No. 4 Bridge Street was occupied by Edward Westall & Son, bootmakers.

A GENERAL VIEW OF ABINGDON FROM THE BRIDGE, c. 1910, looking towards St Helen's Church. (Morland's Brewery)

MARKET PLACE, c. 1890, with the Queen's Hotel (built in 1864) on the right, the new Corn Exchange on the mid-left, and the London and County Bank on the far left. The statue of Queen Victoria was given by Mr E.J. Trendell, a former mayor of the town, in honour of the Queen's Golden Jubilee in 1887. Of these structures only the bank now remains. The Queen's statue was removed to the Abbey grounds after the Second World War, and the other buildings were demolished when the Market Place was redeveloped in the 1960s and early 1970s. (Abingdon School)

INTERIOR OF THE CORN EXCHANGE, probably decorated for Roysse's School Founder's Day celebrations in the 1890s. The foundation stone of the Exchange was laid by the Earl of Abingdon on 11 August, 1885, and the building was completed the following year, at a cost of £3,000. Apart from its agricultural role, it was widely used for meetings and social events. Pevsner described it unenthusiastically as having 'no definite style nor alas any personality.' A new Cattle Market was also constructed as part of the same project. (Abingdon School)

A BIRD'S-EYE VIEW OF HIGH STREET, c.1904, looking west from an upper floor in the County Hall.

HIGH STREET LOOKING EAST TOWARDS THE TOWN (OR COUNTY) HALL, c.1935. On the near left-hand side is the Public Library, opened on 15 April, 1896, by the Earl of Abingdon. During its first year of operation it had the modest total of 3,520 books on its shelves. The Library has now been transferred to the new Charter development and the old building is used as a Job Centre. Pevsner condemned it as 'too tall to be either historically credible or suitable within the scale of Abingdon.'

THE ABBEY GATEWAY, C. 1900. Flocks of sheep were regularly brought into the town for sale at the market well into the present century.

EAST ST HELEN STREET, C. 1920. Pevsner considered it architecturally the best street in Abingdon and that remains true today. St Helen's Church rises elegantly in the background.

ABINGDON. ALMS HOUSES & GARDENS.

LONG ALLEY ALMSHOUSES near St Helen's Church, c.1914. The Almshouses were built in 1446–47 by the medieval Fraternity of the Holy Cross, though they were much altered in the sixteenth and seventeenth centuries. When the Fraternity's endowments became Crown property in 1547 under the Reformation, a new royal charter of 1553 created the body known as Christ's Hospital to administer them and other property belonging to the former Fraternity. It has carried out that role ever since. The Almshouses were intended to cater for six poor men, six poor women, and a nurse.

THE ABBEY, c.1903. The impressive dwelling was then the home of the Hon. Frederick George Lindley Wood, JP.

ABINGDON ABBEY, Gatebrese Chimney.

THE ELEGANT GEORGIAN COUNCIL CHAMBER, c. 1914. It is located on the south side of the abbey gateway, above the Guildhall. Of the oil paintings displayed, pride of place belongs to Gainsborough's *George III* and *Queen Charlotte*, the two large portraits hanging on either side of the fireplace. They were presented by the King to Sir Charles Saxton in 1794, and he donated them to the Corporation in 1808.

THAMES STREET AND THE MILL, ABINGDON ABBEY, c.1930. (Abingdon Museum)

THE GUEST HOUSE OR LONG GALLERY, part of the ruins of Abingdon's famous Benedictine Abbey, which was dissolved by Henry VIII in 1538.

ANOTHER VIEW OF THAMES STREET in the 1930s.

NOs. 2–10 THAMES STREET, as it was when scheduled for slum clearance in 1933. These houses have long since disappeared.

COURT 7, WEST ST HELEN STREET, as it was when scheduled for slum clearance in 1933. The Medical Officer, Dr Sisam, said he had visited these back houses in 1913 and had 'regarded them as unfit for human habitation, and since then they (had) deteriorated.'

COURT 5, WEST ST HELEN STREET in 1933 – another of the back house developments condemned by Dr Sisam.

AT THE JUNCTION OF HIGH STREET AND WEST ST HELEN STREET on the eve of the Victorian era. (Mr D.J. Steptoe.)

THAMES (OR ST HELEN'S) WHARF, c. 1890. The boats on the left perhaps belonged to Gabriel Davis, who in 1891 described himself as launch builder and engineer at St Helen's works.

THE VIEW WEST ALONG OCK STREET FROM THE SQUARE, C. 1875. In front of the obelisk is a weigh-bridge near to where the sheep market was held until the mid-1880s. The war memorial now stands on this site. On the right is the Congregational Church, designed by J.S. Dodd and erected in 1862 to replace an earlier Congregational Church building. It is currently being redeveloped for commercial purposes. (Oxfordshire County Libraries.)

OCK STREET BEFORE THE FIRST WORLD WAR, looking east towards The Square, where the War Memorial was unveiled in 1921. The imposing brick building on the right was originally built by the Tomkins family and is now being redeveloped as offices.

TOMKINS' ALMSHOUSES, OCK STREET, 1907. These were founded in 1733 under the terms of the Will of Benjamin Tomkins, a maltster and a generous supporter of the Baptist Church in the town. They provided accommodation for four old men and four old women and were always closely associated with the Baptist Church. Currently they are being modernised under the aegis of Christ's Hospital and Abingdon Council. (Abingdon Museum)

MOTHERS AND CHILDREN STROLLING IN ALBERT PARK, C. 1910. This park was presented to the town in 1864 by the Governors of Christ's Hospital. It covers about 15 acres. On the north side stands the monument to Prince Albert, the Prince Consort, erected by public subscription in 1865 after a design by Gibbs of Oxford, to commemorate the Prince's untimely death from typhoid about four years before.

Conduit Road looking towards Albert Park Abingdon

CONDUIT ROAD IN THE LATE 1930s, viewed north towards Albert Park. On the right is Trinity Methodist Church, built in 1875 largely through the efforts of John Creemer Clarke. The architect was J. Woodman. Pevsner unkindly describes it as 'full-blown, churchy, with a large N. steeple and fussy Geometrical tracery.'

Park Road, Abingdon

PARK ROAD, C.1914

ABINGDON BRIDGE, with the Nag's Head public house in the background. The bridge was entirely reconstructed in 1929.

THE LOCK.

ABINGDON AS SEEN FROM THE RIVER THAMES IN 1858. The foreground is dominated by the gaol, built between 1805 and 1811, and at this time still used for prisoners. That role ceased in 1868 and six years later the premises were sold. (Abingdon Museum)

THE OLD GAOL YARD IN THE 1930s, with part of the premises converted for use as tenement dwellings. As late as 1934, sixteen families were living there, though this had fallen to eight by 1936, and by the following year they all seem to have been rehoused. In the 1970s the property became virtually derelict but restoration work has recently been carried out and it is now used as a sports and leisure centre. (Abingdon Museum)

ABINGDON BRIDGE, NEAR THE NAG'S HEAD PUBLIC HOUSE, c. 1914, looking towards Bridge Street. No family group would now dare to stand in the middle of the road at this spot!

A WINTRY VIEW OF THE CAUSEWAY, looking towards Abingdon Bridge, c.1914.

TRENDALL'S ROW, THAMES STREET, in 1933 – the year in which it was scheduled for clearance.

NEW STREET, THE VINEYARD, in 1933, the year when it was scheduled for slum clearance. At their meeting in July 1933 the Abingdon Borough Council accepted a tender for the building of 40 Council houses between Caldecott Road and Drayton Road to replace a similar number of houses condemned by the Medical Officer . The then Mayor of Abingdon, Cllr. A.E. Tombs, was an enthusiastic supporter of the slum clearance programme.

STERT STREET BEFORE THE FIRST WORLD WAR. Then, as now, one of the main shopping streets in the town.

THE VINEYARD, c. 1912. The sixth house on the right was the Fox and Hounds public house at No. 66. Its landlord, Edwin J. Welch, was succeeded by Walter Turrell, who remained until the beginning of the First World War. By 1914–15 the premises had ceased to be a public house and were instead occupied by Harry Hazard, a beer retailer. The site is now redeveloped. (Mr M.J. Higgs.)

QUEEN STREET, C. 1900. The narrow entrance into the Market Place remains but the area has now been entirely redeveloped. (Abingdon Museum)

Work and Workplaces

GENERAL VIEW OF MORLAND'S OCK STREET BREWERY before the First World War. (Morland's Brewery)

WORKING AMONG THE BARRELS at Morland's Ock Street brewery, c. 1910. (Morland's Brewery)

MID VICTORIAN COOPERS AT MORLAND'S, probably photographed soon after the firm moved to Ock Street in 1861. (Morland's Brewery)

BOTTLE WASHING AT MORLAND'S BREWERY, C. 1910. (Morland's Brewery)

AMONG THE MASH TUNS at Morland's brewery, c.1910. (Morland's Brewery)

MORLAND'S WORK FORCE, c.1890. (Morland's Brewery)

MORLAND'S UNITED BREWERIES: the Abingdon mineral water factory c.1912. Morland's opened their new soft drinks factory in 1910. (Morland's Brewery)

CELEBRATIONS AT THE END OF FRED HEAVENS' APPRENTICESHIP, On the right is Dan O'Leary, head cooper at Morland's. (Morland's Brewery)

FRED HEAVENS ending his apprenticeship as a cooper at Morland's brewery, Ock Street, after the Second World War. (Morland's Brewery)

CLARKE, SONS & CO.'S CLOTHING FACTORY, West St Helen Street, in 1897. The firm was a major employer of women in the area, with many working in their own home, sewing up garments they collected ready cut out from the factory. The factory workers comprised cutters (always men), sewers, and finishers. The day started at 8 a.m. and ended at 6 p.m., with good timekeeping strictly enforced. As sewers clocked on they collected their thread, which was logged in a book and the relevant amount was deducted from their wages. Pay was on a piecework basis, and an hour was allowed for lunch, between 12 and 1 p.m.

AN OUTING OF CLARKE'S CLOTHING FACTORY WORKERS in the 1920s in front of the West St Helen Street factory. When the firm collapsed in 1932/33 the building was taken over by MG Cars as a store and social club. It was destroyed by fire in the Second World War. The whole of this part of West St Helen Street has now been entirely redeveloped. (Mr D.J. Steptoe)

EXTERIOR OF THE ABINGDON CARPET FACTORY AT THAMES WHARF, c. 1920. The Upper Reaches Restaurant now stands on this site. The Carpet Factory itself succumbed to foreign competition at the beginning of the 1930s. (Abingdon Museum)

SPINNING JUTE AT THE ABINGDON CARPET FACTORY, c. 1920. (Abingdon Museum)

WORKERS AT THE ABINGDON CARPET FACTORY, c. 1900 (Abingdon Museum)

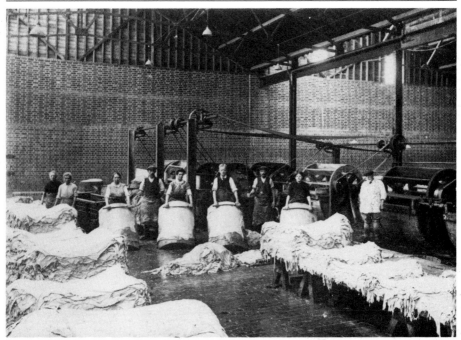

THE PAVLOVA TANNERY DURING THE FIRST WORLD WAR — in the pickle shop at the Spring Grove Works. The Pavlova Leather Syndicate Ltd. opened its Abingdon factory in 1912. During the War the firm had a labour force of between 500 and 600. (Abingdon Museum)

AT WORK AT THE PAVLOVA TANNERY during the 1914–18 War. (Abingdon Museum)

THE MG PRODUCTION LINE in the 1930s when the firm had already established an enviable reputation for the high quality of its sports cars. (Abingdon Museum)

DURING THE SECOND WORLD WAR THE MG CAR FACTORY WORKED LARGELY ON THE ASSEMBLY AND CONVERSION OF TANKS. Many accessories for other tank manufacturers and sets of water-proofing equipment were also produced. Towards the end of the War aircraft work became of increasing importance. The photograph shows men at work on a Crusader tank chassis with a Bofors gun mounted on it. (Abingdon Museum)

THE LAST MIDGET CAR PRODUCED AT MG on 12 December, 1979. It carried a coffin and the message, 'Gone but not Forgotten.' (Abingdon Museum)

CLOSURE OF THE MG FACTORY in October, 1980. The announcement that closure was to take place was made on 10 September, 1979, just as staff were ending the company's Golden Jubilee celebrations. (Abingdon Museum)

MAIDS EMPLOYED BY ARTHUR E. PRESTON, JP at Whitefield, Park Crescent, Abingdon in the mid 1920s. Domestic service was still the principal female employment in Berkshire at this time and in 1931 about half of all females declaring an occupation for the census of population worked as maids. By contrast around one in fourteen was employed as a clerk, typist, or draughtswoman – the kind of office jobs so many women do today. Mr Preston himself had earlier been borough accountant for Abingdon. (Abingdon Museum)

CHAUFFEUR EMPLOYED BY ARTHUR E. PRESTON, JP at Whitefield in the mid 1920s. He was father of two of Mr Preston's maids. (Abingdon Museum)

SUTTON COURTENAY PAPER MILL, c. 1895. Two years later the chimney was demolished, and the mill house itself was turned into a private residence. The mill ceased operation in the early 1880s but in its hey day it had turned out 30 to 40 tons of coloured paper each week. Many of the remaining mill workshops were demolished in the mid 1930s. (Mr D.J. Steptoe)

THE EXPLOSION AT SUTTON COURTENAY PAPER MILL in May, 1869, with part of the boiler embedded in nearby cottages. In one of them an elderly woman was lying ill in bed but the room in which she lay was miraculously untouched. In the other a widow was making her bed when the front of the room disintegrated. However, the section of floor on which she was standing remained intact and she escaped without injury. (Mr D.J. Steptoe)

SUTTON COURTENAY PAPER MILL EXPLOSION on 13 May, 1869. The bursting of the end rag boiler seriously injured three workmen, one of whom subsequently died. Later the debris caught fire and it was with difficulty that the destruction of the whole mill was avoided. John Thomas Norris, the owner, announced that all the workforce would be kept on to help with clearance and rebuilding, and by 1871 the mill was again employing over sixty people in the village. Mr Norris himself died in January 1870, aged 65, and is buried in Sutton Courtenay churchyard. (Mr D.J. Steptoe)

THE DEMOLITION OF SUTTON COURTENAY PAPER MILL CHIMNEY in 1897. A specialist steeplejack from Rochdale was recruited for the job, when it was discovered that the 60-foot high stack was showing weakness at the base. Its fall was arranged along the street. The mill had succumbed to lower cost competition in the early 1880s, but had clearly been in difficulty for some years before closure. When its proprietor, John Thomas Norris, died in 1870, his estate was valued at under £2,000. His widow apparently carried on the business with the aid of a manager until its closure. (Mr D.J. Steptoe)

THOMAS HANKS' COAL WHARF at Sutton Courtenay, c.1900. The barn in the foreground was subsequently purchased by Herbert Henry Asquith, the Prime Minister, as part of the property he acquired when he came to live in the village in 1912. It was converted by Mrs Asquith for use as her private drawing-room and bedroom. (Mr D.J. Steptoe)

THE BRICKFIELD AT CULHAM, c.1884. The Mouldey family owned the brickfield and at the 1871 population census Isaac Mouldey is shown as employing seven men. A decade later he was still in business, aided by at least three sons, though no overall size of labour force was quoted. (Oxfordshire County Libraries)

THE AIR MINISTRY STORES DEPOT at Milton in 1916. Two years later the rector commented on how the Depot had affected village life. 'With the advent of the War,' he wrote 'there started the large Military Depot (RFC) which employed a very large number of the civilians at high wages, even children just left school receiving more than their fathers used to earn. . . . Many families who before the war were earning about 14s a week, (70p) then began to earn as a family £2 to £4 a week (if not more). Moreover in nearly every house lodgers are now taken in and this has seriously affected the religious life of the parish. Many who used to be regular at Church are now bent on making money, and the effect of having so many soldiers in the place has induced many who used to attend church to go for walks, etc.' (Vale and Downland Museum)

THE RAF DEPOT AT MILTON in the 1920s. It is now the site of Milton Trading estate.

ISAAC GERRING AND HIS TWO BROTHERS, wheelwrights and undertakers at Steventon, on 2 August, 1891. Their cottage and workshop stood behind the present school, where the council houses are now built. (Mr W.J. Gerring and Vale and Downland Museum)

HAYMAKING AT LODGE HILL, 12 September, 1926. Throughout the period from 1850 to the outbreak of the Second World War, agriculture was always a major employer of male labour in Berkshire. In 1931 nearly one in four of the county's occupied males worked on the land as farmers, gardeners, farm workers, &c. (Abingdon Museum)

A MIXTURE OF THE OLD WAYS AND THE NEW. A horse team and a tractor working side by side at Milton Hill farm in November 1933.

MECHANIZATION IN FARMING increased during and after the Second World War. Arthur Clifford driving an early combine harvester at Sutton Courtenay in 1951. (Mrs Joan Clifford)

ARTHUR CLIFFORD at work, rick building at Sutton Courtenay, in 1956. He has now worked for the Allen family in this village for well over thirty years. (Mrs Joan Clifford.)

POTATO PICKING remained a labour-intensive activity well into the 1960s in the Abingdon area. An outing arranged in 1951 for 'harvest helpers' on Frank Caudwell's Cross Trees Farm, Sutton Courtenay. (Mrs Joan Clifford)

Shops and Hostelries

ELY BROTHERS,

Newsagents,
Stationers and Tobacconists.

THE BEST SHOP IN THE TOWN
or all Smokers' Requisites, Pictorial Postcards,
Local Arms China, and General Fancy Goods
suitable for Presents.

🌸 🌸 🌸

Note
Address :

42 & 44, Stert Street,
Abingdon~on~Thames.

Near the
Railway
Station.

| Gentlemen's Breeches a Speciality. | | 25 Years Pra Experienc |

W. GERRING

Ladies' and Gentlemen's
Practical Tailor, & General Outfi

Clothes Cleaned, Pressed and Repaired.

12, Bath Street, Abingd

TWO ABINGDON BUSINESSES IN 1907. (Abingdon Museum)

COXETER & SONS, LTD.,

Clincher and Dunlop Tyres Stocked.   Michelin Stockists.

Motor and Cycle Experts

Sole District Agents for
**HUMBER, ARGYLL, DARRACQ,
CLEMENT-TALBOT,
ROVER & SWIFT** **Cars.**

GARAGE. PITS.
ACCUMULATORS RE-CHARGED

Cars for Hire.

Agents for
SWIFT,   SINGER,   ROVER,
HUMBER & RUDGE-WHITWORTH

Bicycles.

Large Stocks of both Motor
and Cycle Accessories.

CYCLE REPAIRS.

REPAIRS BY STAFF OF EXPERIENCED ENGINEERS.

COXETER & SONS, LTD. in 1907. Other branches of the Coxeter business dealt with house furnishings, china, carpet warehousing and furniture removals. The firm was started by Charles Coxeter (1806–1900), who came to the town from Greenham, Newbury in 1820 to be apprenticed to a High Street draper. Sixteen years later he opened a general hardware business in Ock Street and this developed into the firm of Coxeter & Sons, with which he remained closely connected until 1890. When he died in 1900 his estate was valued at the comparatively modest sum of £733 8s 9d (Abingdon Museum)

BAYLIS & CO.'s SHOP AT 5 MARKET PLACE, ABINGDON, in 1901. The poster to the left of the shop advertised Didcot Wool Fair, with '10,000 Fleeces' on offer. That on the right signalled Abingdon Stock Sale – 'Fat and Store Stock' – a reminder of the town's importance as a rural marketing centre. (Oxfordshire County Libraries)

All that is newest for Ladies' and Children's wear at lowest cash prices. Special Department for Underwear and Babylinen. Dressmaking and Millinery a speciality.

This is **CHIVERS', The Leading Drapery House,** 7 & 9, High Street, ABINGDON-ON-THAMES.

Shopping here is a delightful pastime. Visitors will find a splendid selection of presents in the Oriental & Fancy Dept

ADVERTISEMENT BY J. CHIVERS. High Street drapers, c. 1920. Note the offers of Japanese sunshades and boating cushions!

Four Prize Medals against all England. London Dairy Shows, 1889, 1901, 1903.

Specialities:

Well hung Saddles of Mutton.

Spiced Beef, Pickled Tongues, Mild Cured Bacon and Hams.

Bacon and Hams sent carriage paid to all parts.

Note the Address: **J. E. COTTRELL,** Stert Street, ABINGDON-ON-THAMES.

J.E. COTTRELL, BUTCHER, OF 22 STERT STREET, c. 1920. The business had first been established in 1860 and the advertisement of 'Well hung Saddles of Mutton' is presumably confirmed by the large array of carcases hanging outside the shop. This butcher's shop is now occupied by the firm of Hedges.

T. A. RADBOURN, *Telephone 17.*

Fishmonger, Poulterer, & Ice Merchant.
Licensed Dealer in Game.
23, Stert Street, Abingdon-on-Thames.
Prompt despatch of all orders in town and country.   Specialities of
any description.   Established over Half a Century

T.A. RADBOURN'S SHOP C. 1920. Note the generous display of poultry outside – a characteristic of such shops in the nineteenth and early twentiety centuries.

HYGIENIC STEAM BAKERY.

G. F. PALMER,

Bread and Biscuit Baker, - -
Pastry Cook and Confectioner,

Luncheons, Dinners, Teas.
Finest Wines and Spirits.
Bottled Ales and Stout.
Wholemeal Digestive Bread.
28, Stert Street, & 9, Market Place,
ABINGDON-ON-THAMES.

Awarded Special Prize for Hovis Bread, London, 1907.

G.F. PALMER, BAKER, of 9 Market Place and 28 Stert Street, used this advertisement in c.1910 and continued to issue it into the 1920s.

DEPARTMENTS.

Ready-made Clothing.

Hats, Caps, Best Makes.

Woollen Warehouse.

Rainproof Coats.

Shirts, Collars, Ties and Gloves.

Gent.'s Boots, Shoes and Leggings.

Working Men's Clothing of every description.

Hosiery, all kinds of Underwear, &c.

Waterproof Coats, Capes, etc., etc. Umbrellas.

Tailoring, Ladies' and Gent.'s

Tailors' and Dressmakers' Trimmings.

Travelling Bags and Trunks.

E.H. BEESLEY, TAILOR AND OUTFITTER, 22 and 24 High Street, c.1920. The Beesley family's connection with this business began in c.1850 when William Beesley came as a clothier's assistant to Mrs Hannah Harris at her wholesale clothing and drapery store in High Street. When she died in 1883 she left the business to him. However, he only survived her a few weeks and it was left to his wife and three sons to run the firm. Eventually in 1895 the youngest son, Ernest Herbert, took control and the name was changed from Beesley & Son to E.H. Beesley. The firm continued trading until 1984 when the last owner, David Barrett, retired. The shop was then acquired by Hodges, a gentlemen's outfitters from South Wales, under whose name it currently trades.

E.H. BEESLEY'S OUTFITTER'S VAN, C.1910/11. It replaced the firm's old pony and trap and the tailor, Mr Jameson, acted as driver. (Abingdon Museum)

MORLAND'S DELIVERIES to the old George and Dragon public house, Stert Street, c. 1890s. The George and Dragon was completely reconstructed in the early twentieth century. (Morland's Brewery)

THE OLD BELL INN in East St Helen Street prior to its renovation in 1907. It is now known as the King's Head and Bell. (Morland's Brewery)

THE QUEEN'S ARMS HOTEL, formerly the New Inn, c.1863. Described as a Family and Commercial Hotel and Post House, with H. Lindars as landlord. At the beginning of the 1860s the owners, Christ's Hospital, reduced the rent from £100 a year to £75 on account of the poor condition of the property and the fact that many outbuildings were unfit for use. The increasingly shabby state of the premises and of the corner house adjoining it (used as the Rifle Corps Armoury) led to demands for redevelopment of this part of the Market Place. When Christ's Hospital agreed to sell the hotel in 1863, a special limited company was launched to implement that proposal and in September 1864 plans were set in hand to issue £10 shares for the building of a new Queen's Hotel. Its foundation stone was laid the following November by John Tomkins, chairman of the company. (Morland's Brewery.)

Queen's Hotel & Cafe

A.A., R.A.C., N.C.U.)

The Leading Hotel in the District

Best position in fine old Market Square opposite the old County Hall. Two minutes from Station and River. Nearest Hotel to Radley College. Buses leave for Oxford at frequent intervals during the day opposite the Hotel.

Private Sitting Rooms. Electric Light every room **Bedrooms** Hot and Cold Water and Gas Fires. **Billiards.** Garage for 14 Cars.

THE QUEEN'S HOTEL, C. 1937. The hotel was built in 1864 by a joint stock company to replace the old Queen's Arms Hotel, which had previously stood on the site. The Queen's itself was demolished in 1968 when the Market Place was redeveloped. Pevsner described it as constructed of 'red and yellow brick. . . and quite unbelievably joyless.'

COURTYARD OF THE CROWN AND THISTLE HOTEL in Bridge Street, c. 1917. A contemporary advertisement described it as 'replete with every comfort for boating parties, motorists, and cyclists.' It is now a Berni Inn.

THE PLASTERERS' ARMS PUBLIC HOUSE, 39 West St Helen Street, c.1905, with the landlord, George Wm. Enock and his family outside. The Plasterers' Arms disappeared during the mid 1960s, when the area was redeveloped. (Mr M.J. Higgs.)

BRIDGE TEA GARDENS, Abingdon c. 1911 – currently known as the Abingdon Bridge Restaurant.

CALDECOTT HOUSE HOTEL, c. 1937. This was formerly the home of the Hyde family. When its last owner, Major-General Thos. M. Bailie, died in April 1918, the house was converted to a hotel. During the Second World War it was requisitioned by the government. Later it became a Dr Barnardo's Children's Home, before being demolished to make way for a housing estate in 1972. There is a memorial in St Helen's Church to Major-General Bailie and his son, who died in action on the Western front in September 1916.

Transport and Community Services

THE OLD TOLL HOUSE, CULHAM, between the world wars. It was erected following the formation of a turnpike trust in 1736 to improve the 'ruinous state' of the Abingdon to Dorchester road. Tolls continued to be levied until 1875. The house, considerably altered, is now a private dwelling. (Oxfordshire County Museum)

ABINGDON RAILWAY STATION c.1860, with the original 7ft. broad gauge track. At this time the branch line ended in Culham parish, but in 1873, a year after conversion from broad to standard gauge, it was extended a further three-quarters of a mile to Radley. The line was opened for goods traffic on 23 May, 1856, and for passenger traffic on the following 2 June. As a result of its construction, coal prices in the town were sharply reduced from 25s per ton (£1.25) to 16s or 17s per ton (80p or 85p). This particularly benefited the poorer inhabitants. (Mr D.J. Steptoe)

THE GREAT WESTERN RAILWAY STATION at Abingdon, c.1910. The station was rebuilt in 1908, when the previous building was severely damaged by a train! (Abingdon Museum)

ABINGDON SIGNAL BOX — now demolished — c.1930, with the maltings in the background. (Mr M.J. Higgs).

LOCOMOTIVE USED ON ABINGDON BRANCH LINE between the two world wars. (Mr M.J. Higgs).

THE ABINGDONIAN on 23 July, 1963. Empty stock arriving at Abingdon station. Passenger traffic ended on the line in the following September, though it continued to be used on a small scale for freight. The station building was used for some time as a boys' club before being demolished in 1974. (Abingdon School)

ALTHOUGH TRACTORS WERE USED ON BRITISH FARMS DURING THE FIRST WORLD WAR, there was a reluctance to accept them in the post-war period. Here farmers are examining a pneumatic tyred tractor at Milton Hill Farm, near Abingdon, in November 1933.

THE REBUILDING OF ABINGDON BRIDGE in April 1929, to create the present structure. The bridge was formally reopened in September of that year, although traffic was allowed to use it from July. Work began in the summer of 1927.

GETTING READY FOR DELIVERIES ON MAY DAY, C. 1910 at Morland's Ock Street brewery. Until 1913 all deliveries were made by horses or mules; the Abingdon brewery had a stable of 26 horses and mules, while 20 more horses were held at Reading. Some were stationed at depots in Benson, East Ilsley and Faringdon, with goods despatched to the depots as and when needed. (Morland's Brewery)

MORLAND'S UNITED BREWERIES — deliveries on the road, May Day, c.1910. (Morland's Brewery)

MORLAND DELIVERY HORSES outside the cart shed at the Ock Street brewery in October 1936. By this time the firm had acquired a lorry fleet, but horses were still used for local deliveries in Reading and Abingdon up to the Second World War. During the War, with the lorry fleet commandeered, the firm had to revert to horses on a wider scale, and it was not until 1950 that reliance was wholly placed on mechanical transport. (Abingdon Museum)

ONE OF THE FIRST MOTOR CARS TO BE DRIVEN IN ABINGDON, October 1896. It came with a circus and is an early example of a motor vehicle being used for advertisement purposes. (Abingdon Museum)

MORLAND'S LORRY FLEET in the late 1940s. (Abingdon Museum)

A MOTOR BUS CUM VAN RUN BY BARNARD & SON, carriers, c.1922. Harold Barnard is standing in front. It was a foretaste of the motorised era which was to reach fruition after the Second World War. (Abingdon Museum)

THE DRY BED OF THE FORMER WILTS & BERKS CANAL in the early twentieth century. The canal had ceased operation when an embankment collapsed in 1906. The section shown is parallel to Caldecott Road, with Drayton Road in the distance. (Mr D.J. Steptoe)

MEMBERS OF ABINGDON VOLUNTEER FIRE BRIGADE in 1876. The Brigade was formed in 1871, with the corporation agreeing to purchase a Paxton fire engine (see photograph) for around £200. The uniform comprised a helmet, belt and hatchet, and a blouse, for which each member had to pay £1. Where the engine could be dragged to a fire by hand this was done, but if the distance were too great, horses had to be obtained – if necessary by unharnessing them from passing carts and carriages! Agreements were also drawn up with various hotel proprietors for the supply of horses. The first seems to have been made in 1877 with the Queen's Hotel, with the landlord agreeing to supply animals as required for a fee of 30s (£1.50) per fire. (Mr Weir)

ABINGDON VOLUNTEER-FIRE BRIGADE in action at Harwell in 1912 with their steam fire engine, purchased with the help of public subscription in 1905. (Mr Weir)

ABINGDON VOLUNTEER FIRE BRIGADE c.1901 in Roysse's old school yard, which the school had vacated in 1870. In 1901 the Brigade joined the National Fire Brigades Union and brass helmets were introduced to replace leather. In 1881 a two-bay fire station was built in the school yard and remained in use until the early years of the present century. (Abingdon Museum)

ABINGDON VOLUNTEER FIRE BRIGADE members proudly display their new fire pump in February 1933. Standing to the front is the mayor, Cllr. A.E. Tombs, who served as the town's mayor for five successive years during the 1930s.

THE ABBEY GATEHOUSE in November 1858, when in use as a police station. In 1836 the Town Council established a borough force and the gatehouse was then adapted as a police station and inspector's residence. When a new police station was erected in 1865 to the south-east of the gateway, the right-hand arch was unblocked. Also shown is the Russian cannon purchased by the corporation in the summer of 1858 from the Royal Arsenal. It had been captured during the Crimean War and was later moved to Albert Park. By the 1890s police business had been transferred to the county police station in Bridge Street, which is still in use. (Abingdon Museum)

POLICEMEN ON ESCORT DUTY for the mayoral procession in Albert Park between the two world wars. (Mr M.J. Higgs.)

THE COTTAGE HOSPITAL, Bath Street, c.1910. The Hospital was built in 1885–86 on land provided by the governors of Christ's Hospital and was erected largely through the generosity of John Creemer Clarke, the borough's last MP. His wife was one of four ladies to lay foundation stones on 11 August, 1885 – the day on which the foundation stone of the Corn Exchange was also laid. During the year 1911 alone the ten-bed Cottage Hospital treated 95 in-patients and 1,617 out-patients, while 160 more were treated in their homes by the district nurse. The figures are an indication of the value and importance of the service it provided.

THE WARREN, Radley Road, formerly the home of Sir George Dashwood. The house was purchased in 1929 and after conversion was opened as the new Cottage Hospital in the following year. It had four wards, with a total of 24 beds.

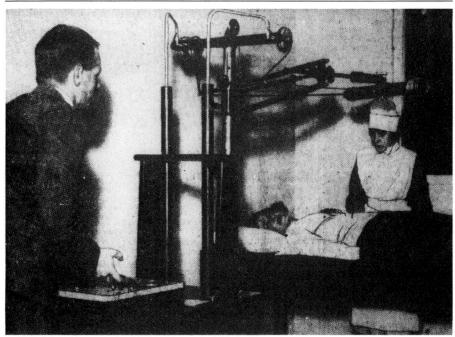

X-RAYING A PATIENT at The Warren in October 1930.

THE FIRST AEROPLANE TO LAND IN ABINGDON arrived in error in January 1912, when the pilot, *en route* from Brooklands to Oxford, lost his way and ran out of fuel. The machine was an Avro and landed in a field along Culham road near the Abingdon football ground. After unsuccessful attempts to re-start it, the machine was dismantled and taken to Shippon, where it was reassembled. The chief pilot of the Avro school, Brooklands, arrived and eventually managed to take off for his home base, only to come down a few miles short of his destination. Subsequently much of the land at Shippon was absorbed by RAF Abingdon. (Abingdon Museum)

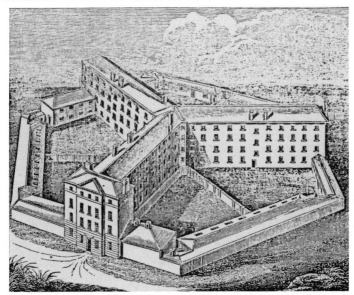

AN ENGRAVING OF ABINGDON WORKHOUSE, opened in October 1835 and built at a cost of about £8,500. It was the first workhouse in the country to be erected under the 1834 Poor Law Amendment Act, a measure designed to make aid to the poor harsher and more cheeseparing than it had been before – hence the prison-like appearance of the whole structure. Its pauper inmates were strictly divided according to age and sex, with parents separated from children, and husbands from wives. The engraving appeared in *The Mirror of Literature, Amusement, and Instruction* in February 1836.

THE FRONT AND MAIN ENTRANCE OF ABINGDON WORKHOUSE, c.1930. In November, 1931, Berkshire County Council decided to close it as part of an economy drive, and on the following 28 December, 20 inmates were transferred to the Wallingford poor law institution. The Abingdon premises then became redundant and about two years later the approximately 12-acre site on Oxford Road, opposite to the Convent, was sold to a Coventry building firm for housing development (Mr M.J.Higgs)

AN AERIAL VIEW OF RAF ABINGDON soon after its opening in September, 1932. (RAF Abingdon).

A XV SQUADRON HAWKER HIND being recovered after a crash landing at Abingdon RAF station in the late 1930s. The young pilot officer in the foreground, with his hands in his pockets, was to become Marshal of the Royal Air Force, the Lord Elworthy. (RAF Abingdon).

Schools and Colleges

AN ENGRAVING OF ROYSSE'S SCHOOL YARD, C.1865. The school traced its origins to a foundation established under Abingdon Abbey in pre-Norman times. But with the dissolution of the parent Abbey in 1538 it fell on hard times, and was refounded in 1563 by John Roysse, a citizen and mercer of London. It was to cater for 63 boys and remained on the same site, south of the Abbey Gateway, until 1870. (Abingdon Museum)

ROYSSE'S SCHOOL (now Abingdon School) pupils in 1865 at their Abbey Gateway site. When the school was inspected by the Schools Inquiry Commission in April 1866 it had 69 boys on the books, of whom 25 were boarders. However, the 'four upper forms had only 15 boys in them.' The headmaster was the Revd William Alder Strange, who held the post from 1840 to 1868. The photograph confirms the youth of most of the pupils. (Abingdon School)

ROYSSE'S SCHOOL (now Abingdon School) in 1874. Four years before it had moved from its cramped sixteenth century site to the current location off Park Road. At the time of the move in 1870 there were only 45 pupils, but by 1907, after fluctuating figures, numbers had risen to over 100, of whom half were boarders. In 1986–87 there were c.700 boys in the school, about 230 of them in the sixth form. (Abingdon School)

ABINGDON GRAMMAR SCHOOL, i.e. Abingdon School, c.1930. The then Roysse's school had moved to its new Park Road premises in January 1870, on land provided by Christ's Hospital. The Revd Edgar Summers was the first headmaster on the new site.

BIG SCHOOL NORTH, Abingdon School, in 1949. After World War Two the school grew in size and reputation under the aegis of the Direct Grant scheme. When that scheme was ended in the 1970s the decision was taken in 1976 to adopt full independent status.

ST HELEN'S HIGH SCHOOL FOR GIRLS c.1930. The school was started in 1903 in a house on the Wootton Road, by the Community of St Mary the Virgin, Wantage, who had already established a similar school in that town. It was intended to cater for the daughters of 'local tradesmen and farmers.' It commenced on 11 May, 1903, with four day girls and four boarders. In May 1904 the foundation stone of the present building was laid by HRH Princess Christian of Schleswig-Holstein and the school moved in about two years later. In 1938 it amalgamated with its sister school, St Katharine's from Wantage.

DORMITORY CUBICLE at St Helen's High School for Girls in the early 1930s. (The School of S. Helen and S. Katharine).

REFECTORY at St Helen's High School for Girls in the early 1930s. (The School of S. Helen and S. Katharine)

BURY STREET NATIONAL (i.e. CHURCH OF ENGLAND) SCHOOL FOR BOYS, *c.*1907. The headmaster was John L. Johnson, MA. The School was built in 1869 for 175 boys, and with similar provision made for girls and infants. It remained on the site until the late 1950s, when the premises were temporarily taken over by North Berks College of Further Education, before the area was redeveloped in the mid 1960s. (Mr M.J. Higgs.)

THE OXFORD DIOCESAN TRAINING COLLEGE FOR SCHOOL MASTERS, c. 1890. The College was built at Culham in 1852, at a cost of £20,000, from designs by J. Clarke. It was opened in January 1853 to train young men wishing to become elementary school teachers and had developed from an earlier, smaller, Anglican training college at Summertown, Oxford, opened 13 years before. Culham College was designed to accommodate 91 students. (Oxfordshire County Libraries).

The Principal (Rev. Canon Ashwell)
Vice Principal (Rev Pickard)
and Masters of Culham College
about 1862.

THE PRINCIPAL OF CULHAM TRAINING COLLEGE with his staff, c.1862. Culham's first principal was a 29-year-old Cambridge graduate, the Revd Arthur Rawson Ashwell, who remained at the college until the end of 1862. He was a stern disciplinarian and during his reign gatings and lines were common punishments for students who misbehaved. Smoking was considered a particularly serious offence!

Oxford Diocesan Training College,
CULHAM.

► General Rules ◄

FOR THE DIRECTION OF STUDENTS IN RESIDENCE.

1. Students must not go out of bounds, except after dinner till the following times :—on Sundays till 6 p.m. ; on Wednesdays and Saturdays till 6.30 p.m. ; on other days till 4.30 p.m.

The whole of the Quadrangle corridor is within bounds, so also is the Lane at the back of the College from the garden gate to the Railway Bridge, and the Eastern front Paddock. Both the Entrance Drives and the School Path are out of bounds. Those parts of the College grounds which are always out of bounds are shown in a plan in the Entrance Hall.

Students must not walk or study in the Grounds or the Lane after dusk.

2. No Student may absent himself from Chapel or Hall without permission of the Principal, or (in his absence) of the Vice-Principal ; nor from Lecture without the permission of the Lecturer. Strict punctuality is required.

3. No Student may go to the Dormitories during the day, except at the hours stated on the notice board, without the written permission of the Vice-Principal, or (in his absence) of the Senior member of the Staff in College.

4. Every Student must retire to his cubicle immediately after prayers at 10 p.m.

No Student is allowed to have a light in his cubicle, except the General Monitor, the Dormitory Monitor on duty and the Bell Monitor. It is strictly forbidden for any Student to enter the bedroom of another at night ; nor may he do so during the day except with the occupant's permission, and when the occupant is himself present.

The lights in the Dormitories are extinguished twenty minutes after retiring ; the Monitors may have their lights till 11 p.m.

Strict order and quietness must be observed in the Dormitories at all times ; no noisy conversation is allowed, and all conversation must cease when the Dormitory lights are extinguished.

Before leaving their bedrooms in the morning Students are required to strip their beds, and to open the window.

No boxes or luggage may be kept in the Dormitories.

5. In the Dining Hall, Lecture Rooms, and Dormitories, the Monitors are held responsible for order, quietness, and neatness, and Students are required to respect and support their authority. No Sporting materials are allowed in any of the College Rooms.

6. All Students are required to take some form of active exercise every afternoon.

7. It is strictly forbidden to enter any Public house for any reason, in Culham, Abingdon or the neighbourhood.

8. Smoking is not permitted in any part of the College buildings, except in the Common Room at stated hours, and in the Hut.

9. Students may not make or retain any acquaintances in the neighbourhood of Culham without the Principal's knowledge and consent.

10. Students are required at all times when away from College, whether in term or vacation, to conduct themselves in an orderly and gentlemanly manner, remembering that the reputation of their College is in their hands.

A. R. WHITHAM,
Principal.

RULES OF CULHAM TRAINING COLLEGE, c. 1900. After undergoing considerable expansion in the 1960s, the College was closed in the summer of 1979 as part of a government rationalisation plan for teacher training. The site was then taken over by the European school, which still occupies it.

CULHAM COLLEGE STUDENTS, c.1864. W.H. Mackett (standing on the far left) taught first at Langley Boys' School, near Slough, when he left Culham at Christmas 1865. He returned to Oxfordshire in September 1868 to become head of Dorchester National (i.e. Church of England) School. He remained there until his health broke over 30 years later. Alfred Pittman (seated on the second row, second from the left) started his teaching career in Edinburgh but then emigrated to South Africa. There he gave up teaching and made a fortune keeping a hotel during the gold rush.

CLIFTON HAMPDEN CHURCH SCHOOL EXTERIOR, 28 November, 1906. The school had been built in 1847 in the ecclesiastical style then popular. (Oxfordshire County Council)

INTERIOR OF CLIFTON HAMPDEN SCHOOL in 1906, showing the older pupils. Note the boys with their Eton collars and the girls in white pinafores. The furniture and fittings were typical of elementary schools in those days.

THE INFANTS' ROOM AT CLIFTON HAMPDEN SCHOOL in 1906, with the mistress, Mrs Creswell. She was wife of the school's head, William T. Creswell, who had come in 1891. He was to remain about 44 years and when he retired Her Majesty's Inspector of Schools paid tribute to the value of his work and especially to his 'distinctive teaching of Science. . . in close correlation with rural and domestic matters.' On the eve of the First World War he earned £115 per annum, while his wife was paid £35 per annum. (Oxfordshire County Council)

STEVENTON CHURCH OF ENGLAND SCHOOL from the Causeway, c.1908.

STEVENTON CHURCH SCHOOL,1920. The teacher on the left is Mrs Annie Gerring. (Mr W.J. Gerring and Vale and Downland Museum)

BURCOT CHURCH SCHOOL was built in 1869 partly as a chapel of ease and partly as a school. Divine service was conducted there each Sunday at 3 p.m. and the schoolroom was separated from the choir of the church by a carved screen. When the photograph was taken early in the twentieth century the headmistress was Margaret E. Thatcher, an uncertificated teacher first appointed in 1899 at a salary of £65 a year. She had about 25 pupils, but was plagued by poor attendance, many of the scholars being kept away for weeks on end to work in the fields. The school was closed in 1922 and the children then attended at Clifton Hampden, about a mile away. Note the impressive motor-car of the Director of Education for Oxfordshire standing outside.(Oxfordshire County Council)

NUNEHAM COURTENAY SCHOOL on 10 June, 1905. It was built in 1849/50 by the Harcourt family and on the eve of the First World War had an average attendance of 48 pupils. The head at that time was John C.K. Russell, who was paid £95 a year. The school was closed in 1960. (Oxfordshire County Council)

CULHAM PRACTISING SCHOOL on 19 December, 1905. The school was opened in 1853 to give Culham College students an opportunity to practise teaching. At first its pupils came from Culham village but by 1904, when it came partly under the control of Oxfordshire Education Committee, it was described as a 'middle-class school', charging fees of 6d to 9d a week. Most elementary schools at that date charged no fees at all. The practising school again started to receive senior boys from Culham village in 1924 but was finally closed in 1931, when the building was taken over by the College itself. (Oxfordshire County Council)

OLDER PUPILS AT SUTTON COURTENAY VILLAGE SCHOOL, c.1950. In 1969 the school was transferred from its old High Street location to the present site in Bradstock's Way. The former school house and school are now private residences. (Mrs P. Steptoe)

ST PETER'S COLLEGE, RADLEY, c. 1900. In the background is the Chapel, first opened in 1895. St Peter's was established in 1847 at Radley Hall, the family seat of Sir George Bowyer. Earlier the premises had been leased by Radley Hall School, a Nonconformist Academy which occupied it between 1819 and 1844. When the new Radley College began it had only 3 pupils, although numbers soon increased. By 1856 there were 133 boys in attendance. In accordance with the wishes of its founder, the Revd William Sewell, DD, it was to give a thorough public school education to upper class boys based on the principles of the Established Church. By 1907 it had a staff of about 20 masters and 226 scholars. In the early days discipline was severe, with beatings frequently administered.

RADLEY COLLEGE BOYS in 1859/60. In the background is the College dormitory. (Radley College)

RADLEY COLLEGE CHAPEL, C. 1903. It was designed by T. Graham Jackson and opened in June 1895. It replaced a small, temporary Chapel used from 1848, which was then demolished. Even today Chapel is regarded as 'the most important building at Radley.'

BOYS LEARNING TO SHOOT at Radley College Rifle Range, before the First World War. (Radley College)

BOYS FROM RADLEY COLLEGE waiting at the local railway station in the 1890s. They were travelling to Henley Regatta, where members of the school were rowing. Prior to the opening of the station in 1873, travellers on the Abingdon line had had to change trains at 'a wretched Junction' exposed to all 'the inclemency' of the weather. (Radley College)

Sports and Recreations

ABINGDON COMRADES FOOTBALL CLUB,1918–20, established at the end of the First World War. (Mr M.J. Higgs)

SUTTON COURTENAY FOOTBALL CLUB winning the North Berks county shield in 1923. During the inter-war years most Berkshire villages had a football team which enjoyed enthusiastic local support. (Mr M. Denton)

River Thames, Abingdon

ROWING ON THE RIVER THAMES, c.1910, with St Helen's Wharf in the background.

River Thames, Abingdon

BOATING ON THE THAMES, c.1900, with vessels hired from James Stevens' boatyard by Abingdon Bridge.

ROYSSE'S SCHOOL FOURS at Nuneham Courtenay in 1870. The School Boat Club, one of the oldest rowing clubs, was flourishing as early as 1840. At that time, and for many years after, it boated from Nuneham, but later moved to Wilsham Road, near the canal basin. (Abingdon School)

ROYSSE'S SCHOOL FOUR, 1897. Sport continues to play an important role in school life, with every boy required to play games at least twice a week. (Abingdon School)

ROYSSE'S SCHOOL REGATTA at Nuneham Courtenay in 1895. (Abingdon School)

ONLOOKERS AT ROYSSE'S SCHOOL REGATTA in 1895. (Abingdon School)

OLD BOY'S CRICKET TEAM, Roysse's School, 1894, including five members of the Morland family and James Townsend, author of a number of histories of Abingdon. He is seated on the far right, wearing a boater. (Abingdon School)

SPORTS DAY at Roysse's School in 1894. (Abingdon School)

A TRANQUIL PICNIC AT NUNEHAM LOCK, Nuneham Courtenay. From the eighteenth century this was a favourite haunt of people from Abingdon and Oxford and a popular subject for artists. During the Second World War, Nuneham Park was requisitioned by the government and in the ensuing period of neglect the lock cottages became derelict.

MEET OF THE OLD BERKS HUNT in Abingdon Market Place around the time of the First World War.

A BOXING DAY MEET in front of the County Hall in 1951. (Abingdon Museum)

MORRIS DANCERS: The Ock Street Horns, in the early twentieth century. According to legend, in 1700 when an ox was roasted in the Market Place a fight broke out between men from the Vineyard and those from Ock Street over the animal's horns. An Ock Street man seized the horns with the aid of a cudgel and they were henceforward used as part of the regalia associated with morris dancing and the election of a 'Mayor' of Ock Street during revels held each June. Recent research casts some doubts on the veracity of the legend, but the horns were certainly used as part of the Ock Street celebrations. From c.1912 to the later 1930s the men seem to have suspended activities, before reviving their morris dancing in 1937. (Abingdon Museum)

ABINGDON MICHAELMAS HIRING FAIR in the 1880s, with the Queen's Hotel, Market Place, in the background. At this date the Fair retained a residual role as an employment exchange for farm workers and domestic servants rather than merely providing amusement and excitement for its visitors – as it was to do in the twentieth century. (Oxfordshire County Libraries)

THE MICHAELMAS HIRING FAIR in the Market Place in October 1930, with St Nicholas's Church in the background.

THE MICHAELMAS HIRING FAIR in October 1951, showing George Irvin's famous galloping horses! (Oxfordshire County Libraries)

Local Events

MORLAND TRANSPORT IN BROAD STREET, taking part in Queen Victoria's Golden Jubilee celebrations in 1887. (Abingdon Museum)

CELEBRATIONS IN THE MARKET PLACE for Queen Victoria's Diamond Jubilee in 1897. According to the photographer, Henry Taunt, 'the National Anthem was sung by the assembled multitude, after which speeches were made, followed by showers of buns from the top of the (County) Hall.' (Abingdon Museum)

QUEEN VICTORIA'S STATUE IN THE MARKET PLACE decorated by the ladies of Abingdon for the Diamond Jubilee in June 1897. The statue was presented to the town by Edwin J. Trendell, a former mayor, in honour of the Golden Jubilee and was unveiled by the Lord Lieutenant of the County, Lord Wantage, on 18 June, 1887. After the Second World War it was removed to the Abbey grounds, where it still stands. (Abingdon Museum)

QUEEN VICTORIA'S DIAMOND JUBILEE CELEBRATIONS in 1897, showing the top of West St Helen Street. Roysse's schoolmasters are in the wagonnette and the boys are on bicycles. (Abingdon School)

PROCESSION OF FLOATS near the junction of West St Helen Street and High Street during the 1897 Jubilee celebrations. In the right foreground Baylis & Co.'s High Street grocery shop is advertising Cadbury's Cocoa, 'Absolutely Pure Therefore Best, no Chemicals Used' and 'Specially Selected Hams, Mild Cure.'(Abingdon School)

PROCESSION OF GOVERNORS, MASTERS AND BOYS OF ROYSSE'S SCHOOL, c. 1890s in High Street. (Abingdon School)

A TUB RACE ON THE THAMES at Abingdon to mark Queen Victoria's Diamond Jubilee in June 1897. Crowds lined the banks and there were marquees and grandstands erected on the meadows. 'All the boats available had been chartered by those who chose that agreeable mode of witnessing the sports,' declared the *Abingdon Herald.*

PROCESSION IN EAST ST HELEN STREET for the Coronation of Edward VII in August 1902. The Coronation had been planned originally for the previous June but the King had had an operation for appendicitis and so the ceremony and attendant celebrations were postponed to 9 August. (Abingdon Museum)

HRH PRINCESS CHRISTIAN LEAVING ABINGDON RAILWAY STATION in 1904 on her way to lay the foundation stone at St Helen's High School for Girls. Princess Helena (1846–1923) was Queen Victoria's third daughter and had married the penniless Prince Christian of Schleswig-Holstein-Sonderburg-Augustenbuerg (1831–1917) in July 1866. They had four children. (Abingdon Museum)

The Visit of H.R.H. the Princess Christian to Abingdon, and the Ceremony of the Laying of the Foundation Stone of St. Helen's School, Abingdon, by H.R.H. The Princess Christian.

On THURSDAY, MAY 26TH, 1904.

Programme of the Proceedings.

1.30 p.m.	The 3rd Batt. of the Royal Berks Regiment will arrive from Churn Camp at Abingdon Station and march to the School Site, (via Stert Street, High Street, Ock Street, Spring Road, and Faringdon Road,) where they will form a Guard of Honour and keep the ground.
2.45 p.m.	The Wantage Troop of the Royal Berks Imperial Yeomanry will arrive at the Railway Station to act as an escort to H.R.H. during her visit to Abingdon.
3 p.m.	A Guard of Honour will be formed at the Railway Station by the Abingdon Company of the 1st Vol. Batt. of the Royal Berks Regiment.
3.10 p.m.	H.R.H. the Princess Christian, accompanied by H.H. the Princess Victoria, and attended by Mrs. W. H. Dick-Conyngham, and Major Evan Martin, will arrive at Abingdon Station, and will be received by the Lord Lieutenant of the County, and the Mayor and Town Council who will present an Address to H.R.H.
3.30 p.m.	H.R.H. will proceed to the site of S. Helen's School, via Stert Street, High Street, Ock Street, Conduit Road, Park Crescent, and Faringdon Road.
3 40 p.m.	H.R.H. will arrive at the School site, being received by the Lord Bishop of Oxford, the Founders of the School, and the Committee, who will ask her to lay the Foundation Stone.
4.10 p.m.	A short service of Benediction will then follow at which the Right Rev. the Lord Bishop of the Diocese will officiate and deliver a short address. In the course of this service the Stone will be laid by H.R.H.
4.40 p.m.	H.R.H. will return through the Town to the Abbey, escorted as before, travelling via Spring Road, Park Road, Bath Street, and High Street.

The Clergy of the Parish alone will wear Surplices.

☞ *It is particularly requested that none of the Visitors should leave their places until H.R.H. has entered her carriage and left the ground.*

UGHER, PRINTER, ABINGDON.

PROGRAMME FOR THE VISIT OF HRH PRINCESS CHRISTIAN to lay the foundation stone of St Helen's High School for Girls in May 1904. (The School of S. Helen and S. Katharine)

THE BERKSHIRE YEOMANRY parading in the Market Place, c.1900. (Abingdon Museum)

THE UNVEILING OF ABINGDON WAR MEMORIAL by the Earl of Abingdon on 11 September, 1921. The Memorial is dedicated to the 'imperishable Memory of our gallant dead,' and records the names of 227 men who had fallen in the First World War (plus those who were killed in the Second World War). In the autumn of 1933 the surroundings of the War Memorial were changed, with six plane trees felled and the fixing of kerbstones around the Memorial itself. (Abingdon Museum)

HM KING GEORGE VI (right foreground) walking away from the back of the Officers' Mess at Abingdon RAF station on 19 July, 1940. He came to inspect No. 10 Operational Training Unit. Two days later the Unit made its operational debut, when three Witley V aircraft each dropped 1,500lbs. of propaganda leaflets over Abbeville, Amiens, Rouen, and Le Havre. They also each took two 250lb. bombs, which were for the secondary task of attacking aerodromes – 'No other target to be attacked.' (RAF Abingdon)

VISIT BY HM KING GEORGE VI, QUEEN ELIZABETH AND THE TWO PRINCESSES to No. 10 Operational Training Unit at Abingdon on 23 May, 1941. (RAF Abingdon)

MID VICTORIAN BERKSHIRE VOLUNTEERS: Fourth Berkshire Rifles, Abingdon Tent No. 2 at Streatley Volunteer Camp. Sergeant Blake is standing in solitary state on the left of the photograph and Corporal Copeland is lying on the grass immediately to the right of him. Volunteer units were recruited in 1859 to combat a threat of war with France. They were retained to the beginning of the present century, when they were merged into the Territorial Army. (Abingdon Museum)

MAYORAL PROCESSION IN EAST ST HELEN STREET between the two world wars. (Mr M.J. Higgs)

SKATING ON THE RIVER THAMES AT ABINGDON during the 'great frost' of February 1895. According to the *Abingdon Herald*, the weather was so severe that hunting and football had to be suspended and 'hockey on the ice' was taken up instead. The minimum temperature readings were lower than 'in any February for forty years.' (Oxfordshire County Libraries)

THE 'GREAT FLOOD' of November 1894 as seen from St Helen's Church Tower. The *Abingdon Herald* of 24 November described it as one of the worst to have occurred in the town during the nineteenth century – 'memory must go back more than seventy years to find a parallel.' In Ock Street the damage was so severe that the mayor distributed special coal tickets to 101 affected householders so that they might each obtain 2 cwt. of coal 'with which to dry their saturated premises.' (Abingdon Museum)

THE 'GREAT FLOOD': Broad Street on 15 November, 1894. (Abingdon Museum)

MAY DAY CELEBRATION in Abingdon in the 1930s. (Abingdon Museum)

AN OUTING FOR THE FAMILY AND STAFF OF E.H. BEESLEY, retail outfitter of High Street, Abingdon, c.1910. (Abingdon Museum)

CLARKE'S CLOTHING FACTORY OUTING, c.1918. (Mrs E. Haynes)

STAFF FROM CLARKE'S CLOTHING FACTORY waiting in front of the Lord Nelson public house, East St Helen Street, to go on an outing in the late 1920s. The Lord Nelson itself was closed in c.1930, although its former landlord, Albert Bullock, continued to live in the house. (Mr D.J. Steptoe)

RADLEY COLLEGE GAUDY, 1894, with parents in attendance. (Radley College)

BRITISH LEGION DINNER in the old Village Hall at Sutton Courtenay during the early 1950s. It was also a birthday celebration; a notice on the back wall reads 'Happy Birthday.' (Mrs P. Steptoe)

SUTTON COURTENAY VILLAGERS IN FANCY DRESS celebrate the Coronation of HM Queen Elizabeth II in June 1953. In the background is the old wooden Village Hall, erected after the First World War. The day began with a procession of villagers and a comic football match and ended with a firework display and bonfire at which 1,000 free 'hot dogs' were served. (Mrs P. Steptoe)

PART OF SUTTON COURTENAY'S CORONATION CELEBRATIONS in June 1953. This tableau was mounted by some of the womenfolk to show the jobs that women took on during the Second World War. Mrs Joan Clifford, driving a Ferguson tractor, is dressed as a member of the Land Army. (Mrs Joan Clifford)

A REMEMBRANCE DAY PARADE at Sutton Courtenay in the early 1950s, with members of the Women's Branch of the British Legion, the scouts and the girl guides. In the background is Rant and Tombs grocery shop – now Sutton Courtenay Provisions. (Mrs P. Steptoe)

Country Houses and Village Scenes

THE VILLAGE GREEN at Sutton Courtenay, c.1904.

SUTTON COURTENAY: Cross Trees 'Triangle', with the Congregational Chapel (now a private house) c. 1919. The foundation stone of this building was laid in June 1907 by the principal of Mansfield College, Oxford, but there had been a Congregational Chapel in the village for many years before that.

THE COURTYARD AT SUTTON COURTENAY MANOR, c. 1914. At this time the Manor was the residence of Capt. H.E.A. Lindsay, who first came to live there in May 1895, shortly after his marriage. Pevsner surmises that part of the house dates back to the thirteenth century, but most was built three or four hundred years later.

ENTRANCE HALL, SUTTON COURTENAY MANOR, c. 1920s. (Oxfordshire County Museum)

HERBALIST'S SHOP in High Street, Sutton Courtenay, c.1900. This became the village post office until 1983. The cottage shown to the left of the shop was demolished in the mid 1980s to make way for 'The Nursery' housing and workshop development. (Mr Carter)

THE GRANGE HOTEL, Sutton Courtenay, c. 1929. This property became an hotel in the 1920s and was owned by County Hostels Ltd. However in October 1929, it was put up for sale, when its amenities included a miniature golf course, tennis courts, croquet and tennis lawns, and a billiard room. By 1931 it was occupied as a private house and its name had been changed to the current one of Lady Place.

THE WHARF, Sutton Courtenay, in October 1915, home of Mr Asquith, the then Prime Minister. He moved to the house in July 1912, after alterations carried out by the architect, W. Cave. Formerly the property had comprised the Queen's Head public house and a neighbouring cottage and Mr Asquith (later the first Earl of Oxford and Asquith) was responsible for the merging of the two properties. His grandson, Mark Bonham Carter, later described the house as an unattractive place which 'could digest an almost incredible number of people in small poky rooms, the largest being the kitchen. The drawing-room . . . was divided into two parts connected by a doorway and a serving hatch, having been in its earlier incarnation the public and private bar. The part beyond the hatch was given over to bridge, the rest was dominated in my memory by a round table on which stood two huge glass jars, . . . one full of bull's-eyes, the other of acid drops.' (Oxfordshire County Libraries)

HIGH STREET, Sutton Courtenay, c. 1916, near the junction with Mill Lane. (Oxfordshire County Libraries)

THE WEIRS, Sutton Courtenay, c.1914.

CULHAM LOCK AND TOLL HOUSE, C. 1884. (Oxfordshire County Libraries)

CULHAM VILLAGE SHOP in October, 1915. Now a private house. (Oxfordshire County Libraries)

PLEASURE STEAMERS by the old rustic bridge at Nuneham Courtenay, c.1910.

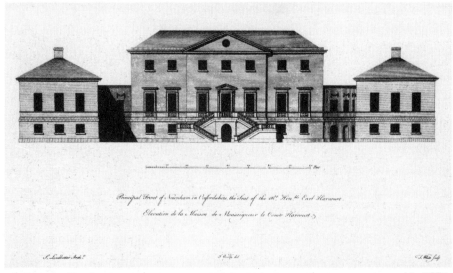

ELEVATION SHOWING THE ORIGINAL PALLADIAN-STYLE DESIGN OF NUNEHAM PARK, engraved in 1771. The house was built for the first Earl Harcourt and plans were already well in hand by the mid 1750s, under the direction of the Eton architect, Stiff Leadbetter, who later built the Radcliffe Infirmary in Oxford. The decision of the first Earl to live on his Nuneham estate involved the removal and rehousing of his tenants from their 'tumble-down clay-built' cottages, as these occupied ground needed for his park and gardens. The wholesale destruction of the old village and its removal to a new site is claimed by some as the inspiration for Oliver Goldsmith's famous poem, *The Deserted Village* (1770)

NUNEHAM HOUSE from the river, c.1900. The elegant Palladian-style mansion built in the 1750s and 1760s for the first Earl Harcourt was altered by his son in the late 1770s and early 1780s. Further changes were put in hand after 1830 by the new owner, Archbishop Harcourt, to produce the house shown in this photograph. Under his direction, the south wing was added to, the mansion's interior was reconstructed, and the east front was remodelled. During World War Two the house was occupied by the Air Ministry and the property fell into a state of disrepair from which it has only recently recovered.

Nuneham Courtenay.

NUNEHAM COURTENAY VILLAGE before World War I. It dates from c.1760, when Earl Harcourt incorporated the old village site into his new park and gardens. The German pastor, Moritz, who visited it in 1782, commented on the 'two rows of low, neat houses, built . . . as regular and as uniform as a London street.' (Mr M.J. Higgs)

The Gardens, Nuneham House.

NUNEHAM HOUSE GARDENS, C.1900. The flower garden was created in the 1770s and 1780s for the Harcourts under the influence of the Revd William Mason, author of *The English Flower Garden* (1781), who was a frequent visitor to the house. With its statuary, grotto, water-garden and Temple of Flora it broke with the landscaping traditions of the day and was widely acclaimed by contemporaries. During World War Two the garden was much neglected but the present occupiers, Rothmans International PLC, are now engaged in its restoration.

LATE-VICTORIAN RADLEY, with the old post office (now demolished) and the church in the background. (Radley College)

MILTON MANOR between the two world wars. The central core of the house was completed in 1663, possibly after a design by Inigo Jones, for the Calton family. In 1764 a London lacemaker and embroiderer named Bryant Barrett purchased the property and added the two wings, as well as the outbuildings. He also extensively altered the interior. The result is a house of great elegance and charm. The elm trees in the photograph were affected by the epidemic of Dutch elm disease in the 1970s and had to be felled in 1976. (Oxfordshire County Music)

THE STRAWBERRY HILL GOTHICK LIBRARY at Milton Manor. It was created by Bryant Barrett and his architect, Stephen Wright, aided by Richard Lawrence, a London carver, and followed a style made fashionable by Horace Walpole's famous battlemented house at Strawberry Hill, Twickenham, in 1747. (Mrs E.J. Mockler)

THE ROMAN CATHOLIC CHAPEL at Milton Manor, completed in 1772. (Mrs E.J. Mockler)

THE RED LION PUBLIC HOUSE, Milton, between the two world wars. It is now known as the Admiral Benbow, to commemorate his association with Milton Manor, which is a short distance away, at the end of the lane. (Oxfordshire County Museum.)

THE DINING ROOM at Milton Manor, with its original eighteenth century decor. (Mrs E.J. Mockler)

THE CROSS ROADS AT STEVENTON, with the War Memorial, c.1920s.

STATION ROAD, STEVENTON, in the early twentieth century. The shop on the left is advertising Colman's Starch, Reckett's Blue, and Quaker Oats.

MILTON LANE, Steventon, in the early twentieth century.

MILTON LANE, Steventon, c.1907. Another view.

THE STOCKS AND WHIPPING POST IN STOCKS LANE, Steventon, in the early twentieth century. (Vale and Downland Museum)

People

THE FIRST EARL OF OXFORD AND ASQUITH at Sutton Courtenay shortly before his death on 15 February, 1928. Herbert Henry Asquith (1852–1928) was educated at Oxford and called to the bar in 1876. He was elected to Parliament in 1880 as Liberal MP for East Fife and served as Home Secretary, 1892–5 and Chancellor of the Exchequer, 1905–8, before becoming Prime Minister in the latter year. He retained that office until December 1916. Created Earl of Oxford and Asquith in 1925, he resigned the Liberal Party leadership in the following year. With him, writes Roy Jenkins in his biography of Asquith, 'died the best part of the classical tradition in English politics.'

THE EARL OF OXFORD AND ASQUITH at Sutton Courtenay with his elder daughter, Lady Violet Bonham Carter, and grandchildren, c. 1927. Lady Violet's son, Mark, recalled that all the children were accommodated in the Mill House, adjoining The Wharf and occupied by the Asquith family from c.1920. He recalled this as a 'delightful house, lit by oil-lamps with a charming walled garden full of hollyhocks and roses.'

BURIAL OF THE FORMER PRIME MINISTER, THE FIRST EARL OF OXFORD AND ASQUITH, at Sutton Courtenay on 20 February, 1928. Somewhat bizarrely, just over a year later his widow obtained special permission for his exhumation and the body was reburied at about 11 p.m. one Saturday night in its present location, approximately 15 yards to the east of the original position. This was done so that the memorial, which Lady Oxford had selected, could be appropriately erected. She herself is now buried nearby.

THE COUNTESS OF OXFORD AND ASQUITH opening a Fête for the benefit of the Village Hall, at the Mill House, Sutton Courtenay, on 23 August, 1930. The Countess is standing in the middle with some of her grandchildren. On her left, slightly to the rear, is Mr Samuel Lewis, a local builder, who was active in village hall affairs and was the father of the photograph's provider. By the end of 1931, shortage of cash forced the Countess to contemplate the sale of her Sutton Courtenay property and in February 1932 The Wharf was put on the market. It was sold early in 1933 and according to her, went 'for a song.' Much of the furniture and other contents of the house were also sold by auction, though the prices fetched were very low. 'I am giddy with fatigue and sorrow over The Wharf,' she wrote to a friend, shortly after handing over the keys to the new owner. (Mrs A.T. Slater)

JOHN CREEMER CLARKE (1821–1895), proprietor of the major nineteenth century wholesale clothing firm of Clarke, Sons & Co. of West St Helen Street. He was also Liberal MP for the borough from 1874 to 1885 and a prominent Wesleyan Methodist. Mr Clarke was born in Devon and began his connection with Abingdon as junior partner in the firm of Hyde, Son & Clarke, clothing manufacturers. The firm specialised in 'slop work,' producing cheap working clothes. It employed hundreds of outworkers in the Abingdon area and was noted in Manchester for its large-scale purchases of cord and moleskin. Mr Clarke lived at Waste Court, Bath Street, where he had a domestic staff of four maids, plus a governess, in the 1870s. At his death his estate was valued at around £85,000, which would make him a millionaire today. (Abingdon Museum)

EDWARD MORLAND (1841–1894), the third son of George B. Morland, an Abingdon solicitor. For some years Mr Morland occupied Rye Farm before becoming head of the brewing firm of Morland & Co. In 1887, when it adopted limited liability status, he became its first managing director. He was mayor of Abingdon from 1892 until his death. Under the terms of his Will almost the whole of his £36,000 estate was left to his solicitor brother, John Thornhill Morland, to administer. (Abingdon Museum)

WILLIAM AND JAMES HEMMINGS, the last of the Ock Street Morris Dancers, in 1910. William (with the melodeon) died in Abingdon Poor Law Infirmary, aged 82, in January 1930 and James in his Ock Street home, aged 80, in January 1935. William was many times elected 'Mayor of Ock Street' and on 5 May, 1910, the brothers took part in a special concert at Kensington Town Hall designed to promote the revival of folk songs and morris dancing. In the nineteenth century their father, Tom Hemmings, had likewise served as Ock Street 'Mayor' for the June revels. (Abingdon Museum)

MRS CAROLINE IRONS OF SUTTON COURTENAY, in 1898. She eked out a tiny living by walking to Oxford and back each week with a handcart to collect meat for sale among the villagers – a journey of over 20 miles. Mrs Irons was the daughter of James Shrapnel, a naval lieutenant, and the great-niece of Lieut.–General Henry Shrapnel, who invented 'case shot.' In 1874 she married Mr Irons, a Wesleyan local preacher, and soon after, they moved to Sutton Courtenay, where he carried on a small butcher's business. On his death in 1879 she took over the business supplementing it with occasional needlework and washing. She lived with her twin sister, Sarah, and a younger sister, Angelina, both of them tailoresses. In 1881, the sisters also had two little girls lodging with them in their Chapel Lane cottage. In 1898 a few charitable friends collected a fund to provide Mrs Irons with an income so that she need no longer make her exhausting weekly journey for meat. She made the last journey on 19 November, 1898. Caroline and her twin sister died on 12 and 11 February, 1901, respectively, aged 75 and were buried in the same grave in Sutton Courtenay churchyard. The photograph shows Mrs Irons with her handcart *en route* from Oxford to Sutton Courtenay in 1898. (Mr D.J. Steptoe.)

THE FORMALITY OF LATE VICTORIAN SOCIAL LIFE IN THE PROVINCES is well exemplified by this wedding photograph of Edward Bathurst Coxeter and Edith Gristwood, in the late spring of 1900 (Vale and Downland Museum)

PHOTOGRAPH CREDITS

The following have kindly provided illustrations and information, or have assisted in other ways, and their co-operation is much appreciated:

Mr A. Brown of Morland's Brewery; Mr T. Carter; Mrs Joan Clifford; Mr M. Denton; Mrs Galloway, deputy headmistress, the School of S. Helen and S. Katharine; Mr W.J. Gerring; Malcolm Graham, Local History Studies, Oxfordshire County Libraries; Mrs. E. Haynes; Mr M.J. Higgs; Mrs Nancy Hood, curator, Abingdon Museum and Vale and Downland Society Museum Centre, Wantage; Mrs E.J. Mockler; Mr A.E. Money, Hon. Secretary, Radleian Society; Radley College; Oxfordshire County Council; Oxfordshire County Museum, Woodstock; Mr M. St John Parker, headmaster, Abingdon School; Flight-Lt. J. Perry, RAF Abingdon; Mrs. A.T. Slater; Mr and Mrs D.J. Steptoe; Mr Weir, Checker Books.